KING'S NORTON

THROUGH TIME

Wendy Pearson

AMBERLEY PUBLISHING

First published 2013

Amberley Publishing
The Hill, Stroud
Gloucestershire, GL5 4EP

www.amberley-books.com

Copyright © Wendy Pearson, 2013

The right of Wendy Pearson to be identified as the
Author of this work has been asserted in accordance
with the Copyrights, Designs and Patents Act 1988.

ISBN 978 1 4456 0833 4

British Library Cataloguing in Publication Data.
A catalogue record for this book is available from
the British Library.

Typeset in 9.5pt on 12pt Celeste.
Typesetting by Amberley Publishing.
Printed in the UK.

Introduction

The south area of King's Norton began the last century with a gradual shift from its rural nature of farms and minor country houses, to small private housing developments. The pace of change quickened following the Great War. After the Second World War the building of massive municipal housing estates on former greenfield sites completely changed the landscape. In the village a number of timber-framed buildings were scheduled for clearance without appropriate consideration of their heritage value. There have been several battles by the community to retain the medieval origins of the village as a focus for the community. The village may be ancient but it is vibrant and responsive to reasonable change.

This pictorial story of King's Norton begins with The Green. The village is the centre for a wide community, which it serves with its shops, open space, and social events. St Nicolas Place is a new name for the collection of the oldest buildings that include the church, Old Grammar School, and Saracen's Head. Following victory in the 2004 BBC Two *Restoration* project a lot of research has been done to reveal the history of the buildings, the village, and the parish. The results of archaeological excavations have provided evidence of the medieval culture of a bustling centre for the wool trade. The tombs and monuments in the church help to provide names for the people who were once active members of the community.

The tour continues around the neighbourhood from where the high-status homes are rapidly disappearing. Many have had a change of use or have been demolished. Primrose Hill Farm and barn have been converted into a care facility, demonstrating the way in which sensitive restoration can return heritage buildings to active life. Photographs from the communities on the larger municipal estates were not readily forthcoming. The industrial area was covered in the sister book *Cotteridge Through Time*. The King's Norton and Northfield Urban District Council did not construct civic buildings like a town hall or museum, but the library, schools, and railway station are indicators of an active administration.

The social activities are loosely connected by gatherings on The Green. Recent Royal celebrations have been followed by street parties. A regular farmers' market on the second Saturday of each month attracts visitors from a wider community. The turning on of the Christmas lights is a popular annual event as is the Church Festival in July. The photographs show the fashions of the period, although some were very hard to date accurately. Some of the less well-known sports are shown by an occasional photograph. There are a number of allotments that generally have a waiting list but any recent competitions from floral and horticultural societies are again unknown. Stories associated with these activities need to be written down before they fade from memory.

King's Norton has an ancient history from Roman times. From the medieval period names start to appear in charters, rolls, wills and in other documents. Three notable early families were the Field's, the Grevis' and the Middlemore's. The late John Hedgland did some remarkable work on the Field family in his study of Primrose Hill Farm. Details of cases adjudicated by Sir Richard Grevis can be found in the records of the Quarter Session Rolls, an example of which is: '8th August 1619. Recognizance before Sir Richard Grevis by John Palmer of Yardley to appear at Sessions to prosecute Francis Swayer for stealing a table cloth and table napkin from Richard Walton of Yardley.' The churchyard monument to the Middlemore's now needs some TLC.

A growing archive of digitised documents is now available on the Internet. The Calendar of Patent Rolls, 21 March 1317, for Edward II (1307–27) records the following:

License for the enfeoffment of William de Haselwell of the undermentioned lands, messuages, mill, etc in Bremesgrove, held in chief, viz., by William Jurdan of Kyngesnorton of a messuage, a carucate of land, 3 acres of meadow and 3 acreas of moor; by Alfred Thekyng of 2 acres of land; by Richard Brademedewe of a mill, 5 acres of land, 3 acres of meadow, and 2 acres of pasture; by Hugh de Cotterugge of a moiety of an acre of moor; by Thomas Jurdan, chaplain, of 32s. Of rent; and by Richard de la Lynde of 5s of rent.

Care is needed when applying these references as there is another King's Norton in Leicestershire. We know from the Domesday Book that King's Norton was one of eighteen outliers of Bromsgrove, which was held by Earl Edwin before the Norman Conquest. Lindsworth was mentioned. Cotterugge is probably a reference to Cotheridge rather than Cotteridge.

King's Norton was frequently part of a marriage dowry and gifted to the new Queen. On 28 September 1697 the manor of King's Norton was leased for thirty-one years to Princess Caroline, dowager Queen. Unfortunately the activities of a Queen are given little attention unless they are the ruling monarch. King's Norton ceased to be a Royal Manor when it was sold to John Taylor II in 1804 for £7,568. He was the son of John Taylor I who was Birmingham's first major manufacturer of buttons and the founder of what became Lloyds Bank.

Industrialisation of the northern part of King's Norton developed along the canals. The junction between the Worcester and Birmingham Canal and the Stratford-upon-Avon Canal opened up the area. This was reinforced with the opening of an 'express' route, via the Lapal Tunnel in Bartley Green, to the Black Country, which was the source of heavy raw materials, especially coal and lime. Small settlements had emerged at Cotteridge and Stirchley. At Bournville, George and Richard Cadbury built their chocolate factory and created the model village. Herbert Austin established his car factory at Longbridge, which expanded rapidly during the Great War and led to him creating a workers village of prefabricated homes imported from America.

King's Norton was a separate administration from Birmingham and was also in a different county, being in Worcestershire rather than Warwickshire. After several years of bargaining, on 9 November 1911, the Greater Birmingham Scheme came into effect. The territory governed by the Councils of King's Norton and Northfield Urban District, and Yardley Rural District, transferred from Worcestershire to Warwickshire. Handsworth Urban District transferred from Staffordshire to Warwickshire. A total of 22,159 acres from Worcestershire and 5,149 acres from Staffordshire were transferred to Warwickshire. This total includes the earlier transfers of Balsall Heath and Quinton (Worcestershire) and Harborne (Staffordshire). The county boundaries that had been created by the Anglo Saxons were changed, and parish boundaries disappeared. Historians need to be aware that earlier records exist under the original county. Studies of Worcestershire or Birmingham pay scant regard to the industrial contribution of King's Norton and Selly Oak.

As Birmingham moved from being a manufacturing centre into a commercial and civic centre for the region, the land occupied by its small independent workshops and the now tired back-to-back courts, was needed for redevelopment. A post-Second World War boom in building municipal housing took place and 8,500 homes were built in the southern part of the constituency which, in 1987, included the Wards of King's Norton, Bournville, Moseley, and Selly Oak. The estates were built speedily and economically but these dream homes soon disclosed structural problems largely through the method and type of construction. The consequent remediation suggests inadequacies in the initial planning and design of the estates, and social isolation problems associated with living in the twenty-four high-rise tower blocks arose. In the last decade parts of the estates have been demolished and rebuilt or are currently scheduled for demolition.

The old photographs are a primary source of historical evidence. There are connections between the pairings of photographs. An attempt has been made to capture the same site as it is today and let the reader identify the changes that have taken place. In other cases a sequence of developments has been recorded. It is important that the memories the photographs may inspire should be recorded before the information is permanently lost. Hopefully the photographs will also encourage a visit to The Green to witness these treasures at first hand.

The Village

The Green, 1920

The Green was once common land where local people grazed their cattle. The attempts to limit public use of the central area by the erection of fences or banning the 'mop' were resisted by the community, who ensured it was retained as open space. During the Second World War, an underground community air-raid shelter was constructed to protect people from bombing raids targeting the factory centre and the Austin motor works. The Malthouse Cottages on the right of the churchyard became Ward's drug store. It had the designated village pump that bore a sign claiming that the water was unfit to drink. This is possibly why the Green had so many pubs! The lych-gate carries memories of the local people who gave their lives in service during two World Wars.

Cottages

The cottages between Bull's Head and Saracen's Head were demolished to build a car park, which is now available for shoppers willing to pay a small charge. A former resident of the cottages remembers finding a significant number of beads in the garden. Evidence of the presence of the cottages can be seen in the side wall of the Bull's Head.

Bull's Head, 1896

The Bull's Head was recorded in 1838 as 'Bull's Head Inn, stable and garden'. The landowner was Richard Francis and the occupier was George Kendrick. It is possible that the building replaced an earlier inn apparently of the eighteenth century. The owner of the Bull's Head in 1901 was Thomas Chaplin. He then sold it to Mitchells & Butlers. It was rebuilt and reopened in 1902. Inside is an attractive tiled staircase typical of an Edwardian design.

West Side Cottages
The small detached cottages at the end of the row were owned by the brewery and used by retired managers. The other cottages have been replaced with shops and offices.

Chas Mann
The Green Gallery once occupied this site. The pet shop has been here for a long time, however it was previously the retail outlet for Chas Mann, whose motorbike shop is now on the west side of The Green. The Green has a long tradition of participation in motorcycle events.

Post Office, 1972

The original post office was near the
library on the Pershore Road. It moved
first to the south side of The Green and
later to its current position on the west
side. Formerly the post office was Evan's
wines & spirits, and later a butcher's
shop. The government's threat to close
it drew a very angry response from the
village and accordingly the post office
has survived.

Old Town Close, 1935

Old Town Close was demolished in 1936 in order to build a cinema. There was substantial local opposition as it was felt a cinema would attract the wrong sort of people to The Green. The cinema, designed by Harold Seymour Scott, opened on 16 September 1938. Television ended the need for cinemas. Films, musicals, local and international news could be seen in the comfort of the home. During the 1960s, 'bingo' evenings were held in a desperate attempt to keep the facility economically viable. The cinema closed in 1983.

King's Norton Cinema, *c.* 1988

When the cinema was scheduled to be demolished, the locals again protested. Kwiksave retail chain acquired it, but planning permission was refused. While the planning committee were conducting a site visit a car crash occurred in front of the cinema, 'proving' the claims that the site was unsuitable for the increased traffic that a supermarket would generate. The interior was described thus: 'the seating and carpeting in both stalls and the small circle was of a light-green colour. Along with the wall lighting, the cinema was lit by a series of decorative grills in the ceiling which stretched the width of the cinema. It had a large orchestra pit at the base of a very imposing proscenium arch, complemented by what seemed huge travellers.' Those who delayed their exit from the car park were likely to find the chains had been replaced and their car was locked in! The Grosvenor Court sheltered housing was later built on the site.

The Plumbers Arms, 1890 and 1912

The Plumbers Arms ceased to operate in 1931. It became a fish and chip shop called Elite Fish Saloon, but in 1968 a fire destroyed the upper storeys. The remaining building became a Chinese restaurant and takeaway, with a barber's shop at the side. The two enigmatic photographs of social outings from the pub suggest they were men-only events.

Excavations, 1992

Excavations at No. 15 The Green were carried out in 1992 by Laurence Jones and Stephanie Ratkai. They discovered evidence of timber-framed buildings from the thirteenth and fourteenth centuries. However, the presence of a large assemblage of twelfth-century pottery suggested earlier settlement on the site and possibly an informal medieval market. From the fifteenth century the area was occupied by gardens until the nineteenth century, when a cellared building was constructed.

Clearances

The watercolour painting was done by A. E. Everitt in 1850. These late medieval buildings were demolished in the 1930s. Excavations revealed sandstone footings of a probably medieval building which lay at the rear of the property facing The Green. Many of the ancient properties had been listed in a schedule for clearances by the Department of Health in 1937. The grounds for this are unknown, and it is questioned whether the person signing the documents was aware that the buildings were much older than the legislation requiring certain standards of construction. The photograph of the King's Norton Electrical Company Ltd was taken in 1937.

Summers Bakery and the Green Laundry, 1890 and 1912

Summers bakery was on the south side of The Green, opposite Grosvenor Court. William Henry Fisher ran the laundry at No. 33 The Green before the cinema was built. The laundry did the washing for the Chamberlain family at Highbury Hall in Moseley, which was in the parish of King's Norton.

Hirons Bakery, 1967
Somewhat unexpectedly this is one of the oldest surviving buildings on the Green. It is a late medieval structure, dating to the early sixteenth century. It is suggested that it was once the home of a chantry priest and was known as St Mary's Hall. It became Hirons bakery in around 1915 and bread was made at the rear of the premises until the 1980s. There are a number of tales of visits from a ghostly figure. It is now a Spar grocery shop. The photograph of the rear of the bakery was taken in *c.* 1930 and shows Mrs Edkins, the owner, as a young girl riding a pony.

The Old Bell Inn, 1907

The Old Bell Inn was owned by Richard Foster, who brewed his own beer. There was extensive stabling behind the inn and a back driveway led from this to the Redditch Road and the Old Mews livery stable. It is possible it was once a coaching inn. In 1896 Richard Foster sold it to Southans brewery, which later sold it to Mitchells & Butlers. The pub was closed in 1931, after which time it was used by a shoe repairer and as a private residence. It survived the Second World War only to become a victim of the blight of demolition that destroyed many of the older houses on The Green.

Twatling, 1937

The east side of The Green was known as 'the Twatling' or 'Twatlings'. The name Twatling is claimed to be an abbreviation of Watling Street, the Roman road. No evidence of Roman occupation has been discovered in the village. Nurse Allen, the village midwife, lived in one of the cottages. The Co-op butcher was replaced by a hairdresser's and a car park for Lloyds Bank.

East Side, 1937

The unexplained clearance process of 1937 caused some of the older houses to be demolished without the land being scheduled for redevelopment. The gap where this building once stood is a vacant plot. The Health Shop on the corner of Back Road has been extended.

St Nicholas Place

St Nicolas' Church, 1980

It is possible that a wooden building predated the present church of St Nicolas. It has a Norman window but the earliest surviving parts are dated to the thirteenth century. There have been many alterations and additions as can be seen from the stonework and reuse of early decorated stone. The Victorian restoration of 1872 was not entirely sympathetic. The church is built on high ground and the crocketed spire forms a landmark that is visible from a considerable distance. The entrance to the tower has a crocketed dripstone and above it a four-light window.

Weather Vane, 1950s

The tower and crocketed spire were built in the fifteenth century. The churches at Yardley and Bromsgrove are of a very similar design, suggesting that the same architect and possibly the same master builders were used for all three churches. There is a story that, when repairs were being done to the spire, the attempt to tighten the fastening of the steel supporting rod resulted in the spire turning. When the weather vane was removed for maintenance Mr Blake allowed local people to pay a few pence to jump over it, a claim they were later able to make once it had been replaced!

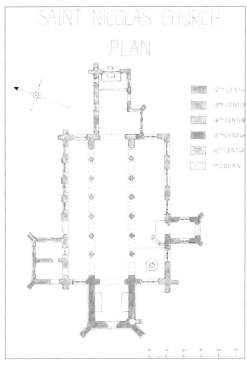

SAINT NICOLAS CHURCH
PLAN

12TH CENTURY
13TH CENTURY
14TH CENTURY
15TH CENTURY
16TH CENTURY
MODERN

Sculptures

The decorative architecture both inside and around the exterior needs to be seen to be appreciated; verbal description does not do it justice. The porch was where marriages and business deals often took place. The sculpture of St Matthew is a 'stringer' at the bottom of one of four ribs that formed the original ceiling. The craftsmanship that went into the designs that can be seen all around the exterior of the church is evident. Architectural terms include corbels, gargoyles, grotesques, and springers. A 'Mass' clock is etched into the wall near the main entrance. Examples of medieval decorated stonework can be seen in the external walls of the chancel.

Chancel, 1844

The nave, including the chancel arch and the north aisle, date from the thirteenth century. There are recesses in the wall that once served as the piscina, ambry and stoop, which were places for washing in holy water and storing sacred objects. The church was the meeting place for religious services, marriages, baptisms and funerals, as well as spiritual guidance and support. The church today also welcomes people for a range of other community activities.

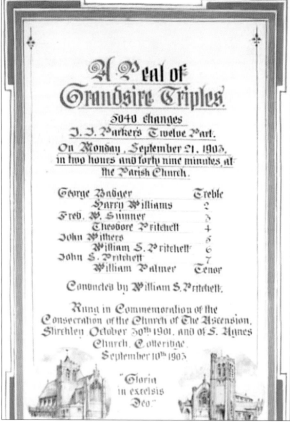

A Peal of
Grandsire Triples.
5040 Changes
J. J. Parker's Twelve Part.
On Monday, September 21, 1903,
in two hours and forty nine minutes, at
the Parish Church.

George Badger	Treble
Harry Williams	2
Fred. W. Sumner	3
Theodore Pritchett	4
John Withers	5
William S. Pritchett	6
John S. Pritchett	7
William Palmer	Tenor

Conducted by William S. Pritchett.

Rung in Commemoration of the
Consecration of the Church of The Ascension,
Stirchley October 30th 1901, and of S. Agnes
Church, Cotteridge,
September 10th 1903.

"Gloria
in excelsis
Deo."

Bell-Ringing

An inventory of 1552 stated that the church possessed four bells. In 1873, a ring of eight bells was cast by Chapman & Mears of London. Two treble bells were added in 1926. In 1903, a world record was set for 'change ringing' without a break. The citation states: 'On Monday May 11 1903 was rung in this tower in a most Excellent Manner a True and Complete Peal of London Surprise Major Containing 14,112 Changes in 8 hours and 40 minutes'. Theodore Pritchett, who became Lord Mayor of Birmingham, was a bell-ringer at King's Norton. The late Ray Adlinton held the post as Master of the Rings and also played the Carillon in Bournville.

Tombs and Monuments

The seventeenth-century tomb of Richard and Anne Grevis was moved from the chancel to the bell tower in the 1870s. He was High Sheriff of Worcestershire in 1609 and Deputy Lieutenant to James I in Wales. The monument shows their eight children. A further altar tomb is to Humphrey Lyttleton and Martha, his wife. She died in 1588 and he survived her until 1624. He is buried in Naunton Beauchamp. It is fortunate that some of the early monuments survived the Reformation, especially as the Revd Thomas Hall, who was a staunch Puritan, would have ensured that the new ordinances were followed. In 1882 a concrete floor was laid in the church and the vaults below were sealed. However, one surviving grave from 1514 is that of Humphrey Toye, a former chantry priest.

Stained-Glass Windows

The window in the chancel is of Norman origin, although the stained glass is Victorian. There are two twelfth-century lancets in the chancel, suggesting that a church was here from at least that time and that the stone building may have replaced an earlier wooden structure. The church has twenty-two stained-glass windows, many of which were made by Hardman's of Birmingham. The fifteenth-century west window and those on either side of the vestry door are of clear glass.

Thomas Hall

The Old Grammar School is visible from the Pershore Road South and accessible from Mirys Lane, the original name for Vicarage Drive. Thomas Hall was curate from 1640 until 1662 and master of the school. The popularity of the school grew and it was attended by pupils from a wide area. Hall was a Puritan and a Parliamentarian in a Royalist stronghold; he became unpopular as a consequence. He wrote a number of treatises and built a considerable library of books, which are now in Birmingham Central Library. He died in 1665 and is buried in the churchyard, although the precise location of his grave is unknown.

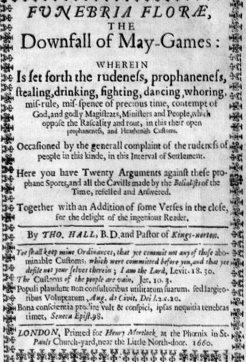

FUNEBRIA FLORÆ,
THE
Downfall of May-Games :
WHEREIN
Is set forth the rudenefs, prophanenefs, ftealing, drinking, fighting, dancing, whoring, mif-rule, mif-fpence of precious time, contempt of God, and godly Magiftrats, Minifters and People, which oppofe the Rafcality and rout, in this their open prophanenefs, and Heathenifh Cuftoms.

Occafioned by the generall complaint of the rudenefs of people in this kinde, in this Interval of Settlement.

Here you have Twenty Arguments againft thefe prophane Sports, and all the Cavills made by the *Beliakifts* of the Time, refelled and Anfwered.

Together with an Addition of fome Verfes in the clofe, for the delight of the ingenious Reader.

By THO. HALL, B.D. and Paftor of *Kings-norton.*

Yee fhall keep mine Ordinances, that yee commit not any of thofe abominable Cuftoms, which were committed before yon, and that yee defile not your felves therein ; I am the Lord, Levit. 18. 30.
The Cuftoms of the people are vain, Jer. 10. 3.
Populi plaudunt non confultoribus utilitatum fuarum, fed largioribus Voluptatum, Aug. de Civit. Dei l.2.c.20.
Bona confcientia prodire vult & confpici, ipfas nequitia tenebras timet, Seneca Epift.98.

LONDON, Printed for *Henry Mortlock* at the Phœnix in St. *Pauls* Church-yard, near the Little North-door. 1660.

29

The Old Grammar School

The Old Grammar School was probably built on the site of houses for chantry priests. The current building is enigmatic in that the timber-framed east window and lower-storey brickwork date from different periods, suggesting the use of valued recycled materials. Theodore Pritchett had bought the building for £10 and presented it to the church. Suffragettes are reported to have broken in with the intention of burning it down, but they fell in love with it and merely left a message in chalk on the board. A contrast in teaching periods is shown by the photographs of the former schoolmaster's desk and chair, and a more recent PowerPoint presentation.

Most at Risk

The opening of a board school resulted in the Old Grammar School becoming redundant and a long period of neglect for the building began. Eventually it was added to English Heritage's 'most at risk' list of ancient buildings. Since 2004 the building has undergone extensive restoration work that has made it watertight and secure from further deterioration. Local school groups are shown how teaching was conducted at the time of the Civil War. The St Nicolas Place website gives details of visiting times.

Tudor Merchant's House and Saracen's Head, 1908

Robert Rotsy, his son Humphrey and grandson Richard were a notable local family. It is suggested that it was Humphrey, a wealthy wool merchant, who built the house close to the church as a display of his status and wealth. Dendrochronology shows that the timber was felled in 1492. During the nineteenth century, part of the building became the Saracen's Head Inn until 1928. Other parts were variously accommodation for the verger, a tea room that had closed by 1931, and a grocery and hardware shop. The restoration project was to emphasise that the original structure of the building built by the Tudor merchant. A complication was that other Victorian parts of the building had historical value, and each change involved specialist debate. The work has been completed and the facility is now enjoyed by many people.

Birdcage Walk

A footpath known as birdcage walk, possibly due to its being enclosed by the trees that met overhead, linked Westhill Road with The Green. Rednal Road was formerly called Pit Lane after the marl pits. By 1885, buildings were appearing on the site of Newhouse Farm. In 1856 two almshouses endowed by the Avenant's charity housed two elderly widows of the parish. These cottages were demolished in 1969.

Parish Hall

A vicarage was built in 1861 and demolished in 1970 when a new vicarage was completed. St Nicolas Gardens was built on the site of the old vicarage. A parish hall was built and opened in 1960. Money had come from donations and various fundraising events. It had a rather unusual roof. Its sale was necessary once the parish office had been established. The retirement development was built by McCarthy & Stone. It was named Awdry Court after the local reverend who created Thomas the Tank Engine.

Neighbourhood

Paper Mill Fields

There were a few houses along what is now the Pershore Road South but had formerly been called Church Hill and School Road. On the one side is the park and on the other the recreation ground, which was known locally as Paper Mill Fields. The fields are a good venue for various sports including cricket and football and they are sometimes used by a travelling fair.

Lloyds Bank

The Ten Acres & Stirchley Co-operative Store (TASCOS) was built in 1936 and included a grocer, butcher, chemist, confectioner and hairdresser. Above the shops is the Co-operative Hall which held public meetings and social events. The hall is now used by the Church of Jesus Christ Apostolic for services and a Sunday school. The white building on the corner has deeds dating to 1845, when it was occupied by Josiah Hands, a cordwainer. He was also the registrar of births, marriages, and deaths, and possibly the postmaster as well. The site has been occupied by Lloyds Bank since 1890, although there have been some major alterations, including changing the location of the entrance. John Taylor, who became Lord of the Manor of King's Norton in 1804, formed a bank with Sampson Lloyd that eventually became Lloyds Bank.

Turnpike Road

The Five Ways junction has changed substantially since the early photograph was taken. The houses in Masshouse Lane and some of those in the centre, including the Methodist Providence chapel, have gone. A traffic island now controls the movement of traffic at this very busy junction. Pedestrians require the services of controlled crossings. Fortunately, when the road became a turnpike in 1830s it bypassed The Green.

Masshouse Farm, 1920, and the Providence Chapel, 1967

It is hoped that someone may come forward with a photograph of Masshouse Farm, as there isn't one in the archives. It is reported that Franciscan fathers held secret masses here during the Reformation. The photograph shows Mr and Mrs Albert Hobbis with their grandson Reginald in the doorway of the farm around 1920. In 1930 the farm buildings were demolished and the land sold to build the Victoria Estate between Wharf Road and Masshouse Lane. The builder and contractor was R. & H. Fletcher Ltd, which claimed its properties were 'unexcelled in the quality of workmanship and materials or in the artistry of their design'. The Methodist Providence chapel was built in 1838, became a newsagent during the First World War, and was demolished in 1978 in order for the junction to be enlarged.

Market Field, 1929

The photograph shows the Navigation pub, the market field and the farm on the opposite side of the road. The rectangular shadow in the air is believed to have been the R101 airship flying towards Longbridge in 1929. Market field was on vicarial glebe land belonging to Revd Joseph Amphlett. Cows were herded up Wharf Road to the market field where Neasom & White held fortnightly sales on Wednesdays. The cattle market was discontinued in 1927.

The Navigation Inn, 1880

The navvies who built the canal often lived in a barracks and used the hospitality of the local pub. The Navigation Inn garden is recorded in 1838 as having stabling, a malthouse and a yard. The landowner was John Rogers and the occupier Thomas Hems. They also owned and occupied the meadow behind, which was called the Lakin, and on which resided a gypsy. The Navigation was partially rebuilt in 1906, although how much of the original building remains is uncertain. A report indicates that the fireplace from the Masshouse Farm was inserted here, although contrary claims say it was installed at the Camp Inn.

Marches Tenement and Holbeche Butcher's, 1937

The building was originally a farm called Marches Tenement. More recently it was where A. J. Holbeche, a butcher, advertised that all sheep and cattle brought direct from the feeders are killed on the premises. After the building was demolished, the site was used for the first TASCOS branch and later as a Christian Science reading room. It is probably the property identified in 1838 as a house, farm buildings and garden owned by Robert Mynors and occupied by George Craythorn. In 1965 it replaced the earlier police station on the Redditch Road. Sergeant Smith, his wife Mary and three children, James, Kevin and Moira, lived at the original police station, which is now a car park.

Wharf Road

In 1838, Sarah Kimberley owned four houses and gardens with unnamed tenants. Further down Wharf Road was a blacksmith on property owned by William Jones. Many of the earlier houses have been replaced with various types of care and sheltered accommodation.

Shephard Family, 1950

The Alpha Farm was the home of the Shephard family of blacksmiths and wheelwrights from 1894 to 1960. The farm is reported to date to the early 1800s and is described as being constructed of oak beams filled in with brickwork. It had a deep well with a wooden pump in the kitchen, a flash oven and brewing coppers. Rowan Court bungalows are now on the site of the farm.

Baptist Chapel

Mary Davenport was the owner of the land on which the Baptist chapel, with its schoolrooms, was built. She also owned four tenements and gardens that were used when the church expanded. Baptisms were carried out in the canal, and on one occasion it is claimed that some onlookers got rather careless during the ceremony and fell in. Apparently Wharf Road was previously named Amphitts Lane after the vicar, who also had property at the top of Parsons Hill. The Worcester & Birmingham Canal Company had a coal and lime wharf, machine house and stable. These were occupied by William Brant, who owned the three houses, one of which was a beerhouse on the canalside.

Baldwin Road, 1908
The corner shop on Baldwin Road at the bottom of Parsons Hill is still retailing. This was known as Massey's shop and was run by C. A. P. Rogers for a number of years. This may once have been a drove road, for moving cattle to the marketplace. A side road has been cut and houses built on the bank behind the shop. Opposite the shop is a small terrace known as Laburnum Cottages.

Cartland Arms

The drive-through McDonalds was once the Sporting Parson, and before that the Cartland Arms. It was named after the local landowning family, which included Barbara Cartland, the writer. Ronald Cartland was killed in action in Belgium serving with the Worcestershire Yeomanry. He was the first MP to be killed during the war.

Parsons Hill

At the top of Parsons Hill is a small parade of shops constructed on what was once a house, offices, stable and garden belonging to Elizabeth Palmer and Suzanna Greves. The occupant was the Revd Joseph Amphlett, and this seems to explain why the road was called Parsons Hill.

Bells Farm

Bells Farm was granted to Hugo de Belne by Edward I for services as an archer. It became part of the Middlemore Estate in the sixteenth century. During the Civil War the Field family were in possession, but there are reports of a family dispute as to which side they ought to support. More recently it was occupied by tenant farmers, until it came into the possession of Birmingham City Council. The building has had a few precarious years with vandalism problems and was nearly gutted by fire. Historically it was an important building, being described as having a house, farm buildings, yards, orchard, garden, moat and foredrove. Behind it the Druids Heath municipal housing estate has been built.

Moundesley Hall

The documented history of Moundesley Hall has sometimes been confused with that of Moseley Hall. It was the family home of Squire Charles Pelham Lane before being bought by Cadbury in 1936/37. The company created covenants to preserve it as part of the permanent green belt. Under an Act of Parliament, Birmingham City Council gained the release of 66 acres to build the Hawkesley Hall and Primrose Hill estates. When Moundesley Hall was being demolished, a sixteenth-century timber frame was uncovered. It is thought to have contained some Jacobean oak panelling recycled from Masshouse Farm and bearing the inscription F/WB 1634. A new Moundesley Hall was built in 1936 and this has now been replaced by a residential care facility. The attractive lodge is Grade II listed, but is now looking rather tired and in need of some attention.

WALKERS HEATH RD
KINGS NORTON

Walkers Heath Farm, 1912

There are still visible signs of former country properties belonging to the gentry along the border with Bromsgrove District Council. This farm has been fortunate to survive and is now in the possession of people who value heritage. The farm and barn are both listed by English Heritage. On the corner of the road and hidden in the bushes is a Victorian fingerpost pointing the way to Headley Heath.

Ellesmere

The tower blocks were possibly built on the site of Ellesmere, a significant property about which little has been written. The house had a large pool, suggesting a connection with Pool Farm. Opposite this is the Walkers Heath Recreation Ground, which is now in the care of a local 'Friends' group. The group has organised a project to bring the grounds back into community use as a park and recreation area. Leanne Youngson recently won the BBC Radio WM Birmingham 'Sports Newcomer of the Year Award'. The remaining building was formerly Headley Fields Farm, which later became Moundesley Park Farm. Features in the landscape may be the remains of farm buildings and a planned garden. The Raybould family had one of two smallholdings on the site.

Goodrest Farm

Goodrest Farm has a tradition of supporting local initiatives and permitting organised groups to use some land for learning country crafts – for example, the Girl Guides visited in 1966. William Pountney rented Goodrest Farm from the Lea family. Through his diaries, Richard Pountney (1804–97) provides an insight into the life of a local farmer. Protection from the cheaper price of imported grain was provided by the Corn Laws, but eventually the farm became uneconomical.

Lilycroft Farm, 1975

Lilycroft Farm, photographed in 1975, is on the edge of the new boundary with Worcestershire. In 1838 it was recorded as Lilly Crofts Farm House, with outbuildings, yards and garden. The landowners then were John Deardon and Susan Staveley, and it was occupied by Richard Arnold. One of the parcels of land was named 'brick kiln piece', suggesting brick-making was taking place in the locality. The Fields Millennium Green has been created on part of the farmland to provide a clean, safe and pleasant green space to be enjoyed by people of all ages and abilities. A good example of a medieval hedge has been protected.

Icknield Street

Excavated livestock compound

Roman Farmstead

It was known that there had been a Roman presence in the area but when the new cemetery was being planned the archaeological excavations revealed some surprising information. A Roman farmstead that had possibly continued after Metchley Fort declined has now been recorded in detail. It is near to the Roman road known as Icknield Street and not far from other signs of Roman settlement at Parsons Hill. The recent photograph shows the potential direct route between this site and the new Queen Elizabeth Hospital, which acts as a beacon for the location of Metchley Roman fort. The steeple of St Nicolas' indicates its proximity The Green, by which travellers may have passed.

Primrose Hill Farm, 1975

Primrose Hill Farm was once called Hole Farm. It was built in the fifteenth century by a member of the Field family. In 1838 the landowner was the late John Brittle, with Thomas Spencer as the occupant. The farm has had a turbulent recent history and in the plans to build a municipal housing estate it was intended that the farm and its barn should be demolished. It was saved from this but had some curious occupants, including a group which reportedly carried out pagan rituals. Fortunately the latest saviours were Chris and Sue Higgins, who have transformed the farm and barns into a sheltered care facility.

Council Estates, 1975

Until the early 1960s, this was meadow and pasture land. The Primrose Hill council estate consisted of several high-rise tower blocks and unimaginative houses, which lack the artistic hand of architects. The roads look somewhat bare of matured trees. The estate was built in haste as a quick-fix solution to provide houses for people relocated from city centre areas. It won an award for good design from the Ministry of Housing & Local Government. The considerable number of requests for transfers from high-rise flats to houses indicates poor satisfaction with properties that restrict community cohesion in the neighbourhood. Structural defects, stemming from the method and type of construction, were identified at Smiths (Wychall Farm Estate); Wimpey No Fines (Primrose Estate); Long Easi-Form (Pool Farm Estate); and timber-framed houses at Hawkesley. Parts of the estates have been demolished and are being rebuilt.

High-Rise Blocks of Flats

The photograph above shows the rapidly constructed high-rise tower blocks that civil engineers may have considered a practical answer to housing shortages. The housing has required long-term and expensive remediation. Two created villages in the same parish, Bournville and the Austin Village, are examples for the world on how to create a thriving community through the living environment, gardens, pathways and open space. What were significantly missing were job opportunities, and retail and community facilities. Only the Bilton industrial estate indicates some planned provision of local jobs.

Pool Farm

The new estate at Pool Farm of three thirteen-storey blocks of flats and fifty houses was built by Morris & Jacombs Ltd. Ellesmere was also in Walkers Heath Road, and its pool was filled in to build an estate with eight-storey tower blocks and other mixed housing. There are few examples of community identity on these estates. Following the 1981 census results, central government identified areas of multiple deprivations in a number of the large council estates, those in King's Norton being named as Pool Farm, Primrose Hill, Bunbury and Pineapple. Unemployment and poor housing were key contributory factors. Statistics show that 60 per cent of the households lived in property rented from the council.

Hawkesley Hall

Richard de Hauekeslowe is listed in the 1275 lay subsidy roll. Earliest spellings give the form 'Hawkeslowe', meaning the Hawk's Hill, which may have a connection with birds of prey. In close proximity to one another were two similar properties, both with moats and both named Hawkesley Farm. An 1864 auctioneer's plan of the estate of Hawkesley Hall identifies it as adjacent to lands of Goodrest Farm, and through which the Wast Hill tunnel runs. It shows the buildings, the remains of a moat, and what may be an ornamental pond, with a long tree-lined drive towards the Redditch Road. An extract from a large-scale undated map states that it is 'Hawkesley Hall on the site of Hawkesley House'. It was clearly a substantial property, but it is still not proved whether this was where Tinker Fox fought a skirmish during the Civil War. The building in the photograph, which dates from the 1970s, is the later hall, which was demolished to build the housing estate.

Hawkesley Mounds

The mounds are 'spoil' from the building of the canal tunnel. Beneath them is an ancient ridge and furrow landscape that dates to the period before the canal was built. Confusion has been caused by the existence of farms at Greater and Little Hawkesley, sometimes expressed as Upper and Lower Hawkesley. The following two statements refer to different developments. At Hawkesley, six-storey flats in loaded brickwork were approved, despite not being reinforced with steel. In 1958 the Lord Mayor opened the Hawkesley Farm Moat estate of three eight-storey blocks of flats.

Redditch Road

Along the Redditch Road are micro housing estates and older large houses. Almost as an adjunct to this, the view opens out to reveal a somewhat barren landscape containing small blocks of flats. Closer scrutiny shows that a number of these are vacant and have been boarded up. There was no immediate explanation as to what the problem was with these properties. People who were relocated here from back-to-back courts lost their community, private space and gardens.

61

Wychall Farm

In 1838 it was described as Witchall Farm and included a house, buildings, yards and garden. The landowner was William Shorthouse and the occupier John Dedicoat. Shorthouse also owned the mill, which included a house, rolling mill, yard, garden and road. Part of the land through which the river passes towards the reservoir has been designated a nature reserve. This includes Merecroft Pool, off Beaks Hill Road. The area is now a wildlife haven supporting a variety of habitats and overseen by the Friends of King's Norton Nature Reserve.

Fairway

The Wychall Farm Estate was a council estate with high-rise towers that have now been demolished and the landscape rebuilt. The estate built on the former golf course is a mixed development with a road through the centre called the Fairway. It has a primary school, community centre and a small parade of shops.

King's Norton Golf Club

The golf club came into existence in 1892, with Austin Chamberlain, MP for East Worcestershire, as president. The professional was David Brown, who six years before had become Open Champion. In 1896, Mr Thomson bought about 70 acres of land, which he rented to the club. The course was acquired by the King's Norton Gold Club Estate Company Ltd in 1900. The club retained its allegiance with Worcestershire even after 1911 when it officially became part of Warwickshire. After the war the club sold a strip of land along the Rednal Road for the construction of prefabricated buildings to ease the housing shortage. The impressive-looking building has survived as King's Norton Bowling Club. The golf club has moved to the new premises in Weatheroak.

Newhouse Farm

Along Westhill Road micro estates have developed from the junction of Westhill Road and Wychall Lane towards the village centre. This was formerly the land of Newhouse Farm. In 1889 the Newhouse estate, by then the property of Mrs S. A. Clarke and Mr J. Thompson, was offered for sale as building land. Each building plot was 24 yards from the road, falling back to a depth of half an acre. From 1946, the Links estate developed off Beaks Hill Road, including Grasmoor Road, Fairmead Rise and Hazelbank.

Canals & Industry

Glen Hurst

Records for what is known as Hurst Mill date from 1221, when it was owned by Roger Clarke. Aaron Jones, whose family owned the mill from the sixteenth century, named his house Glen Hurst. The grinding wheels from 1920 indicate the power of the mill, which remained a corn mill until its demolition. At the end of the Second World War, the mill pool was filled in and a garage built on the site. The mill was used as factory units and the house became first offices, then the building was extended to create the Village Inn and it is now a Toby Carvery. The photograph of the garage is dated as 1996. In 1949 a bus overturned near Camp Lane, injuring thirty-three passengers. A photograph of the accident has a good image of the mill in the background.

King's Norton Business Centre

A number of significant industries developed on the site of the King's Norton Business Centre. In 1859, Thomas Richard Bayliss manufactured cartridge cases here. The company was taken over by Nobel's explosives in 1918, following the death of Bayliss. Nobel's founded the ICI in 1926, and the company was moved to Witton. Five generations of the Heaton family, all with the first name Ralph, were involved in Birmingham metalworking trades. In 1850 Ralph II bought the Soho minting machinery. The King's Norton Metalworks and the Birmingham Mint worked together on a few big contracts, including one to supply the Royal Mint with bronze blanks to be made into coins. Several coins, minted in 1918 and 1919, have a 'KN' below the date making them a collector's item. King's Nortons Metalworks closed after the First World War.

Baldwin's Paper Mill

James Baldwin acquired what was originally part of the Broadmeadow Estate. His papermaking business had outgrown the works in Sherborne Street. At the junction of two canals, it was an ideal location to receive raw materials, especially coal, and to dispatch completed products. He made brown paper for wrapping, blue paper for bags and wadding for guns. Baldwin's paper mill was a steam mill, using water collected in what is now Lakeside Pool.

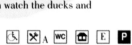
Patrick Motors

The paper mill is now owned by Patrick Motors group, which created the museum known as the Patrick Collection, which displayed vintage cars. The advertisement dates to 1993. Lack of interest in the museum made it unsustainable and some of the cars have been sold to provide funds for research and support for muscular dystrophy patients. Alexander Patrick has recently been rewarded with a CBE for this charitable work, which has contributed £6 million to the cause. Recently, Jones the butcher's van, from the television programme *Dad's Army*, was sold at auction for £63,100. The collection of cars has been reduced to about fifty vehicles and is only open by appointment.

King's Norton Brickworks

This letter to the War Office in 1916 shows a perspective image of the brickworks. The earliest known dates for the brickworks are surprisingly recent. It required 10 million bricks to build the Wast Hill Tunnel, and the local Brandwood (Shakespeare) and Lapal Tunnels also required a lot of bricks. Where were they all made? Clearly local clay was available, but there are few indications of where any earlier industrial-scale brick-making processes were being carried out.

Brickworks Kiln

The owners of the brickworks, the Atkins brothers, brought in the Hough family to upgrade the company. Alan Rollason was appointed manager and the company continued until 1958. It produced 200,000 bricks each week and a further 20,000 on Saturdays. If they didn't meet the target, the men had to work overtime. During the Second World War, the Germans are reported to have been ordered not to attack the site because the tall chimneys provided a substantial landmark feature to enable bombers to attack the Austin Motor Company at Longbridge. Since the works was demolished, the site has remained vacant due to the gases produced by the decomposing domestic waste that was used to fill in the pool.

Guillotine Lock

The Guillotine Lock was constructed in 1802 and has just undergone a restoration procedure that required the closure of the Stratford-upon-Avon Canal. The toll-keeper's cottage and stables have gone, and the road bridge has been replaced. The purpose of the lock was to make the canal boat users pay their fees. Originally there had been a slight difference in height between the waters of the two canals that met at King's Norton. The locks were put there to control the water flowing from one canal to the other.

Junction House, 1972
The Junction House was constructed in AD 1796, according to the legend visible on the building. A number of purposes have been ascribed to the building, which was primarily accommodation for canal officials to collect tolls from cargo barges. The tariffs are clearly displayed on a board on the building. There was a Junction Inn, but whether it was here or near the Guillotine Lock is debated.

High Bridge

The former bridge over the canal in Masshouse Lane was known as High Bridge. It was proposed to replace this with a bridge that could accommodate two-way traffic and improve bus access to the housing estates. Work was scheduled to start in 1992. Bridges can be important features for identifying ancient routes. Features like clapper boards show crossing places over small streams that may indicate a packhorse track, and some bridges remain as unexplained features in fields.

Wast Hill Canal Tunnel

The tunnel, which is known locally as the 2-mile tunnel, was projected in 1791 and completed to Hopwood in 1797. The tunnel digging was done by manual labour. Shafts were dug at various stages, and navvies were lowered down to work in both directions. The engineering was so good that the tunnel was straight enough to be able to see a small patch of light at the far end. Initially the canal boats were 'legged' through the tunnel, often by youths, who received chocolate crumb if it was a Cadbury delivery. Pairs of donkeys were used to pull the vessels, and they were walked across the land to the other end of the tunnel. From the 1870s, steam tugs hauled strings of narrowboats through the tunnel.

Tunnel Cottages

In 1964 tragedy struck when two teenagers on a canoe expedition capsized and died. Their bodies were recovered by frogmen. Another fatal accident occurred in the 1980s when repairs were being done to the inside of the tunnel. Above the tunnel, two cottages were built for those charged with overseeing the use of the tunnel. These are now listed and dominated by the estate that has been built up around them.

Public Buildings

Unification with Birmingham, 1911

Before unification with Birmingham, the King's Norton & Northfield Urban District Council built libraries and other public buildings in Northfield, Selly Oak, Cotteridge, Stirchley and King's Heath. There are claims of fierce opposition to unification with Birmingham, yet in a poll taken in 1909 only 38 per cent of ratepayers bothered to vote. Apparently 3,628 people voted against it and 1,764 people voted for it. Regardless, the scheme was put to Parliament and much of the parish of King's Norton was transferred to Warwickshire. Records for King's Norton up to 1911 are under Worcestershire.

KING'S NORTON RATEPAYERS
SHOULD POLL FOR
UNIFICATION WITH BIRMINGHAM
BECAUSE

Worcester spends 4/- out of every £1 paid by King's Norton in rates.

King's Norton cannot be free from Worcester without union with Birmingham, unless it obtain separate incorporation.

Separate incorporation means ever-increasing rates.

Unification will give all the advantages of separate incorporation at little or no expense.

King's Norton's local patriotism is towards Birmingham.

King's Norton's civic interest is in Birmingham.

King's Norton has no individuality without Birmingham.

King's Norton will have 16 representatives on the City Council—twice as many as it now has on the County Council.

King's Norton will have the moral support of 40 representatives from the outlying districts, and of 23 City Councillors, who now reside in such districts.

All these will voice the needs of King's Norton more powerfully than 8 out of 84 on the County Council.

The Tramway difficulties will disappear by substituting one controlling authority for several with conflicting interests.

Longer tram stages with cheaper fares will inevitably follow. King's Norton cannot work the trams at a profit.

Birmingham successfully governs from one centre the Gas, Water, Tramways and Sewerage for more than 1,000,000 people.

Birmingham has many assets which relieve the rates 1/- out of every 9/-.

Unification means true Home Rule, instead of Worcester Rule.

Unity is strength and amalgamation produces economy.

VOTE FOR UNIFICATION
AND SAVE THE EXPENSE OF SEPARATE INCORPORATION.
PERCIVAL JONES LIMITED, PRINTERS, 98-99, GREAT CHARLES STREET, BIRMINGHAM.

Public Library, 1906

The library was built next to the post office in 1906, funded by a grant from Andrew Carnegie. The foundation stone was laid by Counciller Edwin Shephard. The building was designed by Benjamin Bower and built by Mr Jackson at a cost of £1,000. It contained a junior section, newspaper reading room and reference book reading room as well as a lending department. The foundation stone was laid by Edwin Shephard, a member of KN&N UDC. The library was enlarged in 1939, with alterations to the north side of the building and the use of land at the rear that had been a garden. An essential car park can't be built on land beside the library because of the historical ridge and furrow farming that is evident there.

The Workhouse, 1930s

The building in the centre of the photograph was the workhouse until a new one was built at Selly Oak, which later became the hospital. After the transfer of inmates to the new accommodation, the building was used as rented accommodation for families before being demolished in the 1930s. The land remained waste for nearly twenty years before houses were built on the site. The building on the right of the workhouse was the Village Institute, where adult education classes took place.

Railway Station, 1907

This postcard, taken from Middleton Hall Road in 1907, shows the railway station overlooked by the church spire. The station is famous as the origin of the Thomas the Tank Engine stories. The Revd Awdry began telling the stories to his son Christopher. In a project to differentiate street art from random graffiti, pupils from the King's Norton Boys' and Girls' Schools were given the opportunity to design the story of King's Norton past and present, which was then applied professionally to the footbridge on Station Road. The Middleton Hall Estate was described by the Birmingham Freehold Land Society in 1895 as a very select development, designed to attract the professional classes. It was on a former coach road and laid out with fifty plots either side.

Board Schools, 1890

The Education Act of 1870 required board schools to be set up in areas where the church schools could no longer cope with the numbers of pupils. An office for the school board was established and this is now the Green Nursery. Schools for boys, girls and infants were built. Attendance at the school was often affected by the seasonal demands of haymaking, harvesting and even gathering fruit.

Junior and Infant Schools, 1906
When the schools became oversubscribed, the Old Grammar School was used as an annex. The opening of Cotteridge School eased the problem. The schools score highly at OFSTED inspections and an example of their music was heard at an annual festival of the church.

King's Norton Mixed Secondary School

King's Norton Mixed School was built in 1958 as a large secondary modern school with good external facilities. As an Institute of Further Education it provided evening classes for adults. It was closed and reopened after refurbishment as Cadbury Sixth Form College. Following the reorganisation of secondary education in Birmingham, this was one of three sixth form colleges set up in 1983. It attracts students from a wide area and has a considerable number of feeder schools. The number of students on roll varies from 1,350 to nearly 1,500.

St Thomas Aquinas Roman Catholic School
When the Wychall estate was opened, junior and infant schools were provided, but these became oversubscribed when the estates at the Middleton Hall Road end of the parish were completed. The site was used as an annex until 1963, when it was demolished to make room for St Thomas Aquinas Roman Catholic Secondary School.

Primrose Hill School

The former Primrose Hill School was renamed King's Norton High School, and it has now undergone a further major change and become Ark Kings Academy. No photograph was forthcoming of the earlier buildings, but mention has been made of the former sports hall, which had an interesting roof. The new buildings certainly look attractive. The adjacent primary school has become Ark Rose Academy. The wind turbine in the grounds attracts attention.

Leisure & Entertainment

King's Norton Fair, c. 1890 and 1937

In 1616, James I granted King's Norton the right to hold a market on Saturdays; two fairs, one on the Vigil of St Mark and the two days following, the other on 5 August and the two days following; and a statute fair on the first Monday in October. From the late nineteenth century the statute fair became a fairground or village fête. It was revived for the coronation of Queen Elizabeth II and members of the King's Norton Round Table took over the running of the event, which continues today and for which The Green is closed to traffic.

The Mop, 1963

The Mop was formerly a statute or hiring fair where employers could recruit workers. Each person seeking a job would display a symbol of their trade. Perhaps the name indicates that there was a significant need for domestic service. Inevitably there developed an anti-mop protest, possibly because of difficulties associated with the meeting of people from the city with those of the country. The location of the Mop changed from The Green to Town Field behind the Old Square. It changed again to the Lakin behind the Navigation Inn. The ox roast was carried out on the sale ground, which is now the car park of the Navigation pub. The photograph from 1963 depicts Mr Clayson of the *Birmingham Post and Mail* taking a ride with 'Miss King's Norton' – Rita Bird of Alvechurch Road.

King's Norton Park

The park was laid out after the village's unification with Birmingham. It offered a bowling green, putting green, tennis courts and cricket or football pitches. It also offered sheltered quiet areas of grass and flower beds. The main entrance is very impressive. Mr Markham was the park-keeper for many years. The changing rooms and glasshouses have now gone, and a new skateboard facility has been erected to occupy the local youths, while a small playground entertains younger children. At one time there were prefabricated houses along Westhill Road, but these much loved residences were demolished and the occupants rehoused.

Village Band, 1901

This is a very old photograph of the village band. King's Norton Prize Band won the Gisbourne Silver Challenge Cup in 1911/12. There have been other adult bands associated with the village but these stopped when many of the men went overseas during the First World War. It was therefore rather pleasant to find that a junior band had been formed and was participating in one of the festivals held on The Green.

Bank Holiday, 1908

The Green was a place where people would congregate on special occasions or holidays. They could listen to the band, have a picnic and engage in some of the various social or recreational activities provided by the village pubs or the church. Coronations were also celebrated with a mass turnout of villagers. Apart from trying to identify what the people were doing or wearing, look at the buildings and the roads and paths. A farmers' market is now held on the second Saturday of each month.

Festivals

This was a children's party in front of the Bull's Head. The entrance to the pub was moved to the front in 1902 when the Bull's Head was rebuilt, suggesting that the photograph was taken before this date. The new photograph was taken at an annual church fête in July.

Youth Fellowship, 1950s

The King's Norton Youth Fellowship was formed in 1949 when the Revd Ashford challenged a group to run a club under their own jurisdiction for a trial period of three months. John Hill and Philip Haycock accepted the challenge, formed a committee and got on with the project. The focus was not simply on entertaining its members but supporting their education and well-being. It produced a magazine called the *Spire*. The group were very successful, evidenced by the 117 members who sat down to a three-course Christmas meal. The church is the centre of many community activities, and the churchyard is opened to run charitable events to raise money for local needs.

Celebrations, 1945

The end of the Second World War was marked with street parties. The recent royal wedding between Prince William and Catherine Middleton has seen many of these being held across the country. Perhaps the biggest festival shared universally is Christmas. The lighting of the tree is a community event. Marcia Greenwood, the Ward Support Officer, is sorting out the generator to ensure a successful switch-on of the lights.

Individual Sports

The Golf Club had a very successful ladies membership including full members, life members, non-playing members and junior members. The photograph of the rifle club has already aroused interest, although the venue and origins are currently unknown.

Football, 1918/19

Mary Smith originally worked for Lever Brothers at Port Sunlight, one of the company's garden villages. She played in the football team before marrying James Smith, who became Police Sergeant and lived in the station on Redditch Road. It was a surprise to see that women were playing organised competitive football at this period, and their team outfit is an incredible record of female sports clothing. The Pilkington's male team were playing a match at the former Triplex ground. In the background is a bowls match.

Acknowledgements

A book about a community involves the input of a considerable number of people and the following is a list of the groups who have made a contribution.

The local history group: Frances Hopkins; Pauline Childs; Brian Bates; Peter Marshall; Myra Dean; Piers Morgan; Dorothy Pearson; Moira Smith; Maureen Dixon and the visiting guests.

The King's Norton History Society: Claire and Richard Simpson; Liz Roberts; Malcolm Beach; and many other members including Ron Clements, and Ian Walters. James Melling, who has written informed studies of the church, Saracen's Head, Old Grammar School, and the Junction House. Talks for the King's Norton History Society take place on the last Monday of the month.

The staff at King's Norton Library and Birmingham Central Library, including Patrick Baird of the Local Studies Department, who have all given support and shown interest in the way the community has been involved.

Recent studies by historians Stephen Price and George Demidowicz are substantial works for reference. Their detailed report following the historical and archaeological study of The Green includes the contribution of Malcolm Hislop and others. The reports of archaeological excavations by Alex Jones, Josh White, and Bryony Halstead contributed our knowledge of the Longdales Road site. Laurence Jones and Stephanie Ratkai produced a report on No. 15 The Green in 1992. Dr Mike Hodder and Professor Carl Chinn have both ensured that interest in the history of King's Norton is shared.

Thanks are owed to the late Helen Goodger whose book has provided an authoritative basis for continuing studies, and Kath Watts who has made available her extensive collection of photographs. Writers of local studies that haven't been published include: C. A. P. Rogers; Janet Hourigan; Val and Brian Fletcher; Maurice Robinson; and Rachel Bannister. General contributors are: Mark Norton; Graham Thompson, Andrew Maxim; Tom Hill; and Alton Douglas.

It is very difficult to identify the authors of the original old photographs as frequently copies of their images have become part of other collections. I apologise for the use of any photograph for which the author has not been contacted for their consent.

The final thanks go to Amberley Publishing, and especially Joseph Pettican, for making this book happen.

Bibliography

Helen Goodyer, *King's Norton* (1990); George Demidowicz and Stephen Price, *King's Norton – A History* (2009); Reverend Alan White, *The Worcester and Birmingham Canal – Chronicles of the Cut* (2005); Carl Chinn, *One Thousand Years of Brum* (1999); Michael Hodder, *Birmingham – The Hidden History* (2004); Anthony Beaumont-Dark, *Selly Oak Constituency Plan* (1987); Herbert Manzoni, *Report of the Survey* (1952); Wendy Pearson, *King's Norton Past and Present* (2004); Pauline Caswell, *King's Norton* (1997).